Dear Reader,

We're excited to introduce you to this w   our
Beginnings collection.

Scientific curiosity begins in childhood. Exp   animals and their environments—
whether in nature or in a book—is often at the root of a child's interest in science.
Young Jane Goodall loved to observe the wildlife near her home, a passion that inspired
groundbreaking chimpanzee research. Charles Turner, pioneering entomologist,
spent hours reading about ants and other insects in the pages of his father's books.
Marine biologist, author, and conservationist Rachel Carson began writing stories
about squirrels when she was eight. Spark curiosity in a child and watch them develop a
lifelong enthusiasm for learning.

These beautifully illustrated, information-packed titles introduce youngsters to the
fascinating world of animals, and, by extension, to themselves. They encourage children
to make real-world connections that sharpen their analytical skills and give them a
head start in STEM (science, technology, engineering, and math). Reading these titles
together inspires children to think about how each species matures, what they need to
survive, and what their communities look like—whether pride, flock, or family.

More than a simple scientific introduction, these animal stories illustrate and explore
caring love across the mammal class. Showing children this type of attachment in the
natural world fosters empathy, kindness, and compassion in both their interpersonal
and interspecies interactions.

An easy choice for the home, library, or classroom, our Beginnings collection has
something to spark or sustain budding curiosity in any child.

Enjoy!

Dia

Dia L. Michels
Publisher, Platypus Media

Beginnings

P.S. Our supplemental learning materials
enable adults to support young readers
in their quest for knowledge. Check them out,
free of charge, at PlatypusMedia.com.

Cuddled and Carried

Consentido y Cargado

By Dia L. Michels
Illustrated by Mike Speiser

Platypus Media
Washington, D.C.

My mama grooms me

Mi mamá me limpia

and guides me.

y me enseña.

My mama cuddles me

Mi mamá me da calor

and carries me.

y me carga.

My mama snuggles me

Mi mamá me mima

and shelters me.

y me abriga.

My mama nurtures me

Mi mamá me cuida

and nuzzles me.

y me acaricia.

My mama nourishes me.

Mi mamá me alimenta.

My family loves me very much.

Mi familia me da mucho amor.

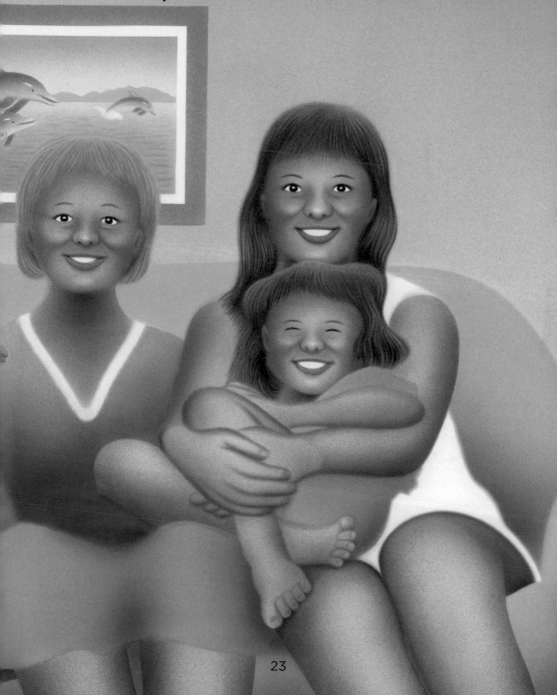

Cuddled and Carried • Consentido y cardado [stroller bag edition]
ISBN 13: 978-1-930775-65-7 | ISBN 10: 1-930775-65-2 | October 2019
eBook ISBN 13: 978-1-930775-79-4 | eBook ISBN 10: 1-930775-79-2 | October 2019
Part of the Platypus Media collection, Beginnings
Beginnings logo by Hannah Thelen, © 2018 Platypus Media

Written by Dia L. Michels, Text © 2019
Illustrated by Mike Speiser, Illustration © 2019

Cover and Book Design: Hannah Thelen, Platypus Media, Silver Spring, MD
        Holly Harper, Blue Bike Communications, Washington, D.C.
        and Linsey Silver, Element 47 Design, Washington, D.C.
Transadaptation: Victory Productions, Worcester, MA
Back Matter Translation: The Spanish Group, Washington, D.C.
Spanish Language Consultant: Edgardo Moctezuma, Latin American Book Source, Inc.

        Originally published in a larger size | June 2018
        Hardback ISBN 13: 978-1-930775-96-1 | ISBN 10: 1-930775-96-2
        Paperback ISBN 13: 978-1-930775-95-4 | ISBN 10: 1-930775-95-4
        eBook ISBN 13: 978-1-930775-97-8 | ISBN 10: 1-930775-97-0

Teacher's Guide, available in English and Spanish, at the Educational Resources page
of PlatypusMedia.com

Published by: Platypus Media, LLC
        725 8th Street, SE
        Washington, D.C. 20003
        202-546-1674 | Toll-free: 1-877-PLATYPS (1-877-725-8977)
        Info@PlatypusMedia.com | www.PlatypusMedia.com

Distributed to the book trade by: National Book Network
        301-459-3366 | Toll-free: 1-800-787-6859
        CustServ@nbnbooks.com | www.NBNbooks.com

Library of Congress Control Number: 2019901689

10 9 8 7 6 5 4 3 2 1

Printed in Canada.

Dia L. Michels is an internationally published, award-winning science and parenting writer who is committed to promoting attachment parenting. She has authored or edited over a dozen books for both children and adults. She can be reached at Dia@PlatypusMedia.com.

Mike Speiser's artwork has been featured on the covers of *Wild Animal Baby* magazine and in the Leigh Yawkey Woodson Art Museum. He is involved with efforts to protect the natural world for future generations. He can be reached at Mike@PlatypusMedia.com.

Victory Productions provides translation, assessment, and curriculum services. The Victory team of native linguists and content specialists uses proprietary tools and pedagogical expertise to meet language needs. Visit them at www.VictoryPrd.com.

What Do We Call Them?

	Animal Name *Nombre del animal*	
	English • *Inglés*	Spanish • *Español*
cover	Bobcat	Gato montés
p. 2-3	Goose	Ganso
p. 4	Panda	Panda
p. 5	Wolf	Lobo
p. 6	Manatee	Manatí
p. 7	Dolphin	Delfín
p. 8	Orangutan	Orangután
p. 9	Koala	Koala
p. 10-11	Sea Otter	Nutria del mar
p. 12	Elephant	Elefante
p. 13	Seal	Foca
p. 14-15	Snow Leopard	Leopardo de las nieves
p. 16	Penguin	Pingüino
p. 17	Flamingo	Flamenco
p. 18-19	Fox	Zorro
p. 20	Polar Bear	Oso polar
p. 21-23	Human	Humano
p. 25	Cougar	Puma

¿Cómo los llamamos?

Baby Animal Name / Nombre de la cría		Group Name / Nombre colectivo	
English • Inglés	Spanish • Español	English • Inglés	Spanish • Español
Cub	Cachorro	Clowder/Clutter/Pounce	Manada
Gosling	Polluelo de ganso	Gaggle	Bandada
Cub	Cachorro	Group	Colonia
Pup	Cachorro	Pack	Jauría
Calf	Ternero	Aggregation/Herd	Colonia
Calf	Delfinato/Cría de delfín	Pod	Vaina/Grupo/Manada
Baby/Infant	Mono	Troup/Buffoonery	Colonia
Joey	Osito koala	Population/Colony	Población/Colonia
Pup	Cachorro	Raft	Manada
Calf	Ternero	Herd	Manada
Pup	Cachorro	Pod	Manada
Cub	Cachorro	Leap	Manada
Chick	Pollito	Colony	Colonia
Chick	Pollito	Flamboyance/Stand	Bandada
Cub	Cachorro	Skulk	Jauría
Cub	Cachorro	Celebration	Colonia
Baby	Bebé	Community	Comunidad
Cub	Cachorro	Pack/Pride	Manada

Animal Classes
Clases de animales

ACTIVITY: Using these definitions, match each animal pictured in the book to its correct class. Which classes appear more than once? Which do not appear at all?

ACTIVIDAD: Usando estas definiciones, empareja cada animal en la imagen del libro con su clase correcta. ¿Qué clases aparecen más de una vez? ¿Cuáles no aparecen en absoluto?

Bird / *Pájaro*

An animal that has wings and is covered with feathers.

Ex. eagles, robins, flamingos

Un animal que tiene alas y está cubierto con plumas.

Ej. águilas, petirrojos, flamencos

Reptile / *Reptil*

An animal that is cold blooded, lays eggs, and has a body covered with scales or hard parts.

Ex. turtles, crocodiles, snakes

Un animal que tiene sangre fría, que pone huevos y tiene el cuerpo cubierto con escamas o partes duras.

Ej. tortugas, cocodrilos, serpientes

Fish / *Pez*

An animal that lives in water and has gills and fins on their body.

Ex. goldfish, carp, sharks

Un animal que vive en el agua y tiene branquias y aletas en su cuerpo.

Ej. pez dorado, carpa, tiburones

Mammal / *Mamífero*

An animal that has hair/fur, is endothermic, has a backbone, and feeds milk to its young.

Ex. horses, dogs, humans

Un animal que tiene pelo/pelaje, que es endotérmico, tiene una columna vertebral y alimenta a sus pequeños con leche.

Ej. caballos, perros, humanos

Amphibian / *Anfibio*

An animal that can live both on land and in water. When they are first born, they have an aquatic gill-breathing larval stage before typically developing into a lung-breathing adult.

ex. frogs, toads, salamanders

Un animal que puede vivir en la tierra y en el agua. Cuando nacen, tienen una etapa de larva en la que respiran por medio de branquias en el agua antes de desarrollar típicamente los pulmones adultos.

Ej. ranas, sapos, salamandras

Arthropod / *Artrópodo*

An animal that has more than four jointed legs.

Ex. bees, spiders, crabs

Un animal que tiene más de cuatro patas con articulaciones.

Ej. abejas, arañas, cangrejos

Answers

Respuestas

Bird Class / Clase de pájaro:
goose/ganso, penguin/pingüino, flamingo/flamenco

Mammal Class / Clase de mamíferos:
bobcat/gato montés, panda/panda, wolf/lobo, manatee/manatí, dolphin/delfín, orangutan/orangután, koala/koala, sea otter/nutria del mar, elephant/elefante, seal/foca, snow leopard/leopardo de las nieves, fox/zorro, polar bear/oso polar, human/humano, cougar/puma

29

Care and Attachment
Cuidado y Apego

Mothers care for their babies in many ways. Each animal baby has different needs based on their habitat, how fast they grow, and the social behavior of their species. Scientists identify four categories of care for mammals.

ACTIVITY: Review the definitions provided here and try to match the mammals in this book to the way the mother cares for her babies.

Las madres cuidan a sus bebés de muchas formas. Cada animal bebé tiene necesidades diferentes de acuerdo a su hábitat, con la velocidad con la que crecen y con el comportamiento social de su especie. Los científicos identifican cuatro categorías de cuidado para los mamíferos.

ACTIVIDAD: Revisa las definiciones proporcionadas aquí e intenta emparejar a los mamíferos en este libro con la forma en la que la madre cuida a sus bebés.

Cache / *Esconder*

Ex. deer, rabbits / *Ej. venado, conejos*

HINT: There are no cache mammals in this book.

PISTA: No hay mamíferos que escondan a sus pequeños en este libro.

Follow / *Seguir*

Ex. giraffes, cows / *Ej. jirafas, vacas*

HINT: Look for babies that walk or swim by mom.

PISTA: Busca bebés que caminan o nadan cerca de su mamá.

Nest / *Anidar*

Ex. dogs, cats / *Ej. perros, gatos*

HINT: Look for animals snuggling together.

PISTA: Busca animales que están acurrucados.

Carry / *Cargar*

Ex. kangaroos, humans / *Ej. canguros, humanos*

HINT: Look for babies that are often held, or hold onto mom.

PISTA: Busca bebés que a menudo son cargados por su mamá.